Crawly Creatures

CENTIPEDES

GAIL RADLEY

BLACK RABBIT BOOKS

Bolt is published by Black Rabbit Books
P.O. Box 3263, Mankato, Minnesota, 56002.
www.blackrabbitbooks.com
Copyright © 2020 Black Rabbit Books

Marysa Storm, editor; Grant Gould, designer;
Omay Ayres, photo researcher

All rights reserved. No part of this book may be reproduced, stored in a retrieval system or transmitted in any form or by any means, electronic, mechanical, photocopying, recording, or otherwise, without written permission from the publisher.

Names: Radley, Gail, author.
Title: Centipedes / by Gail Radley.
Description: Mankato, Minnesota : Black Rabbit Books, [2020] | Series: Bolt. Crawly creatures | Audience: Age 9-12. | Audience: Grade 4 to 6. | Includes bibliographical references and index.
Identifiers: LCCN 2018019418 (print) | LCCN 2018021579 (ebook) | ISBN 9781680728156 (e-book) | ISBN 9781680728095 (library binding) | ISBN 9781644660201 (paperback)
Subjects: LCSH: Centipedes–Juvenile literature.
Classification: LCC QL449.5 (ebook) | LCC QL449.5 .R33 2020 (print) | DDC 595.6/2-dc23
LC record available at https://lccn.loc.gov/2018019418

Printed in the United States. 1/19

Image Credits

Alamy: blickwinkel, 22; Panther Media GmbH, 23; commons.wikimedia.org: Ashley Dace, 29; Duk, 3; EnDumEn, 28; Dreamstime: Mriya Wildlife, 26–27; Taechit Tanantornanutra, 10; Tim Hester, 6 (centipede); Getty: TOM MCHUGH, 17; iStock: CSA-Plastock, 1; jungledragon.com: APR CC0, 20–21; Science Source: NATURE'S IMAGES, 22–23 (btm); Shutterstock: AndrewASkolnick, 4–5; aSuruwataRi, 14 (sink); Evgeniy Ayupov, 24 (insects); fivespots, 12–13 (bkgd); GlebSStock, 6 (bkgd); Henrik Larsson, 24 (spider); Hintau Aliaksei, 24 (toad); irin-k, 24 (centipede); JAAOJA, 11 (top); khlungcenter, Cover; Kristel Segeren, 11 (btm); kzww, 24 (worm); Mauro Rodrigues, 22–23 (btm); Melinda Fawver, 14 (centipede); moj0j0, 12–13 (silhouettes); Narupon Nimpaiboon, 15; Pakhnyushchy, 24 (rat); photomaster, 24 (bird); PISUTON'c, 31; sarocha wangdee, 18 (inset); SherSS, 18 (large); Siriporn Schwendener, 28–29; yothinpi, 8–9; zaidi razak, 32
Every effort has been made to contact copyright holders for material reproduced in this book. Any omissions will be rectified in subsequent printings if notice is given to the publisher.

CONTENTS

CHAPTER 1
Meet the Centipede......4

CHAPTER 2
Where They Live
and What They Eat.....10

CHAPTER 3
Family Life............19

CHAPTER 4
Their Roles
in the World...........25

Other Resources..........30

CHAPTER 1

Meet the CENTIPEDE

It's nighttime. Centipedes crawl out from under rocks and leaves. They move on many legs, hunting. A juicy insect would make a tasty meal. One of the centipedes senses a fat bug. It strikes, tangling the insect in its legs. A quick jab from its poison claws makes the **prey** helpless. It's dinnertime!

5

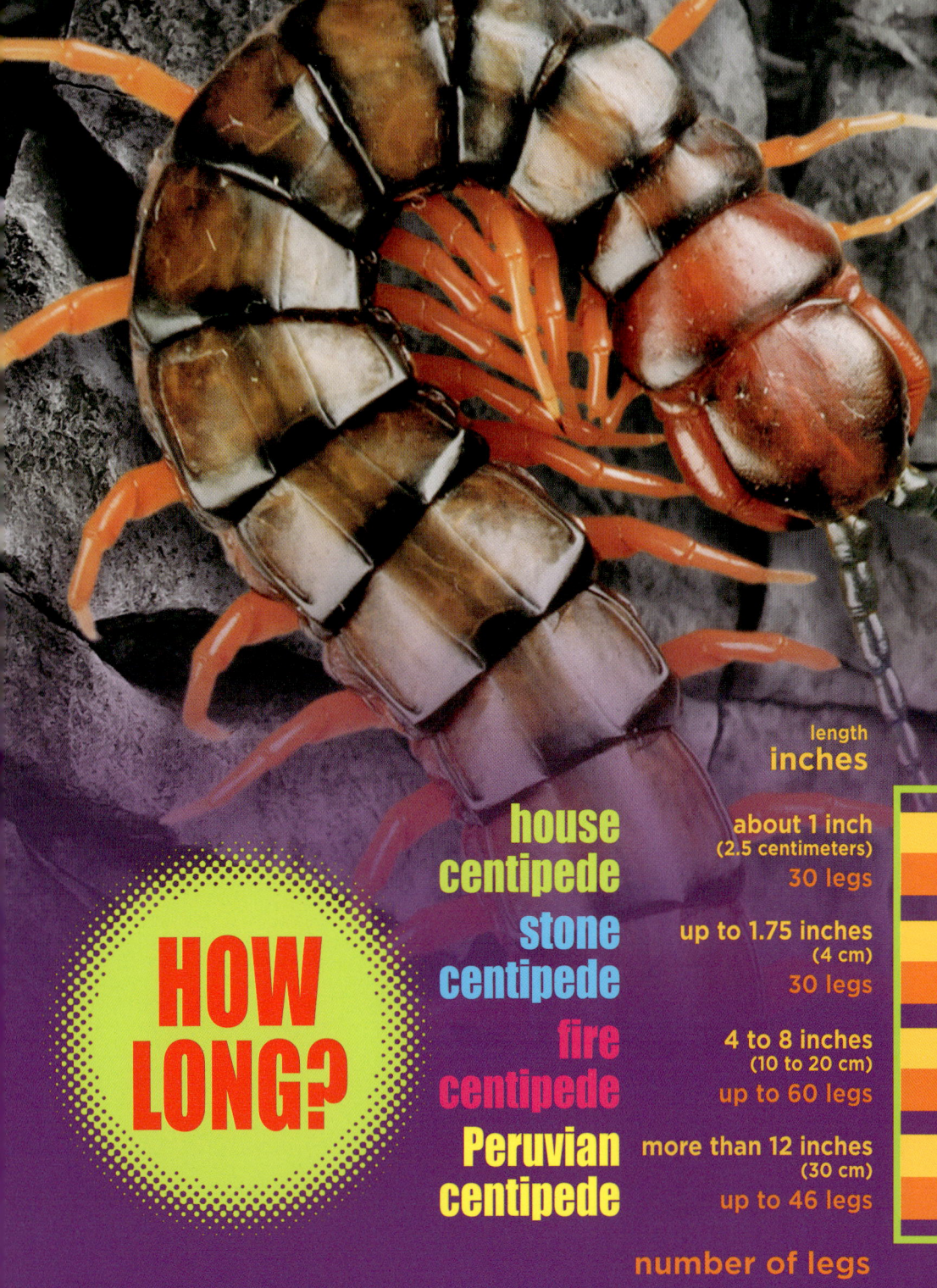

HOW LONG?

	length inches	
house centipede	about 1 inch (2.5 centimeters) 30 legs	
stone centipede	up to 1.75 inches (4 cm) 30 legs	
fire centipede	4 to 8 inches (10 to 20 cm) up to 60 legs	
Peruvian centipede	more than 12 inches (30 cm) up to 46 legs	

number of legs

There are about 3,000 known types of centipedes. They come in many sizes.

All Those Legs

Centipedes are crawly creatures called **arthropods**. Arthropods have body parts made of **segments**. Each segment has a pair of legs. Centipedes have 15 to 177 pairs of legs. They have poisonous claws behind their heads.

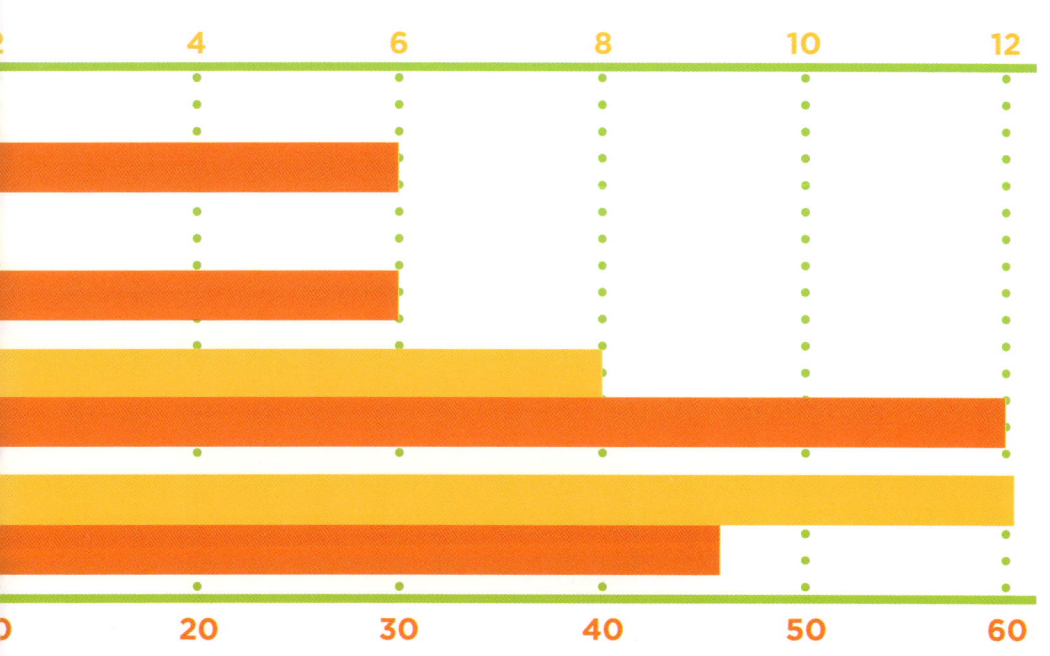

CENTIPEDE FEATURES

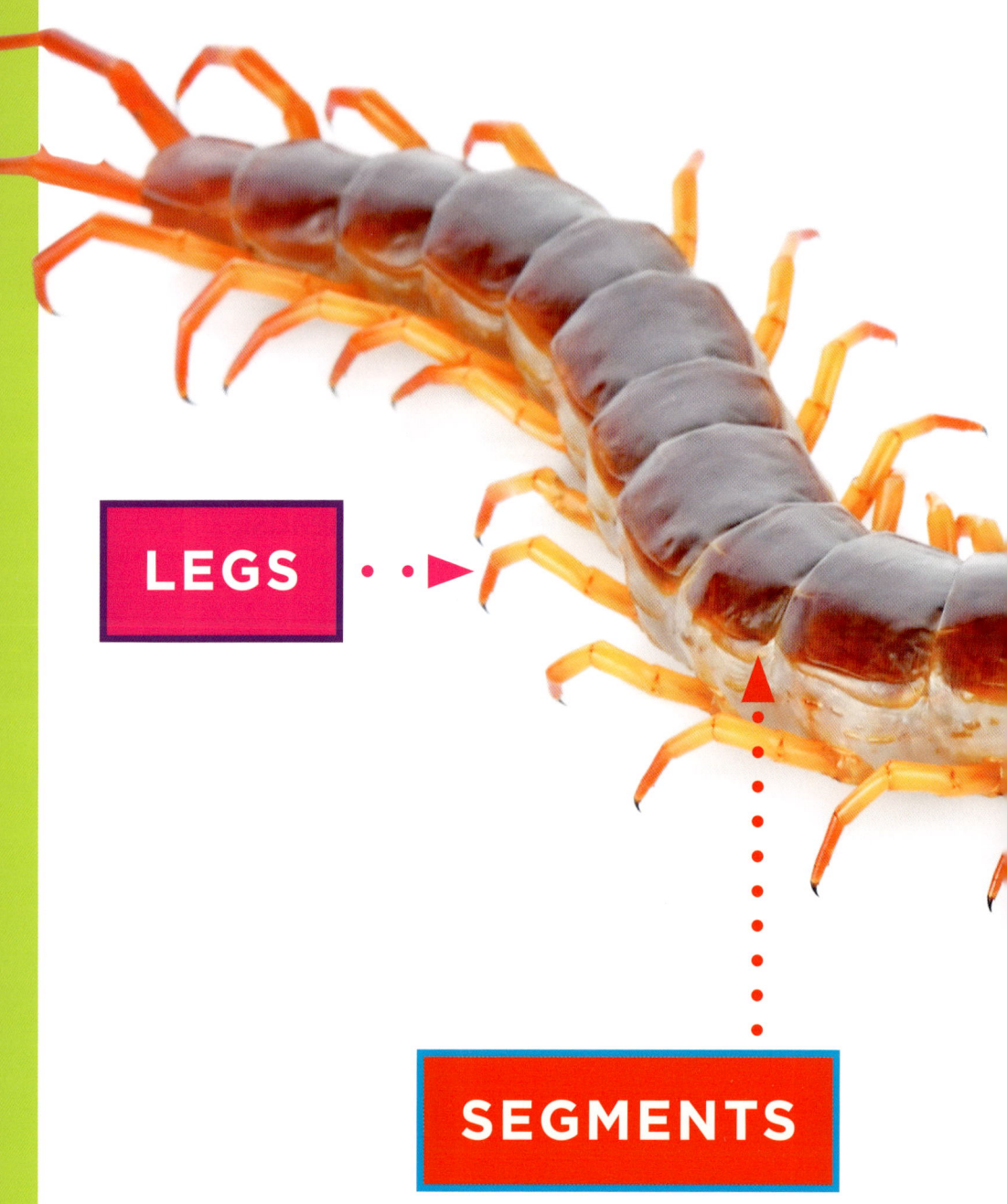

LEGS

SEGMENTS

SPIRACLES

ANTENNAE

HEAD

POISONOUS CLAWS

9

CHAPTER 2

Where They Live
and What They Eat

Centipedes live around the world. They like it damp, dark, and dirty. **Compost**, dead leaves, and loose bark make good homes. They are great hiding places from **predators** too.

Other Centipede Hideouts

under stones

cracks in walls

beneath logs

CENTIPEDE RANGE MAP

Centipedes live on every continent except Antarctica.

In the House

House centipedes live in people's homes. They like damp bathrooms and basements the best. They hunt for bugs while people sleep. If surprised, the centipedes run away.

In 2016, scientists reported a swimming centipede. It's about 8 inches (20 cm) long.

On the Hunt

Centipedes are mostly nocturnal. They leave their homes at night to hunt. Many centipedes have poor eyesight. Some have no eyes at all. They find prey using touch and smell.

Most centipedes eat bugs. But larger centipedes can go after much bigger prey. Centipedes use poison to kill their meals.

Most centipede poison is harmless to humans. But some can cause pain, fever, and swelling.

Not all centipedes
care for their eggs. Some centipedes leave their eggs. Others even eat them.

CHAPTER 3

In warm weather, female centipedes lay up to 60 eggs. Some species curl around the eggs to protect them. They clean the eggs so **fungi** doesn't grow on them. Other centipedes give birth to live young.

Eggs often develop in a few months. Young centipedes are called **nymphs**.

19

Growing Up

Centipedes have **exoskeletons**. Nymphs shed them as they grow. This process is called molting. Most centipedes grow more legs with each molt.

Centipede LIFE CYCLE

Female centipedes lay eggs.

Most centipedes are fully grown in two to three years.

Centipede Food Chain

This food chain shows what eats centipedes. It also shows what most centipedes eat.

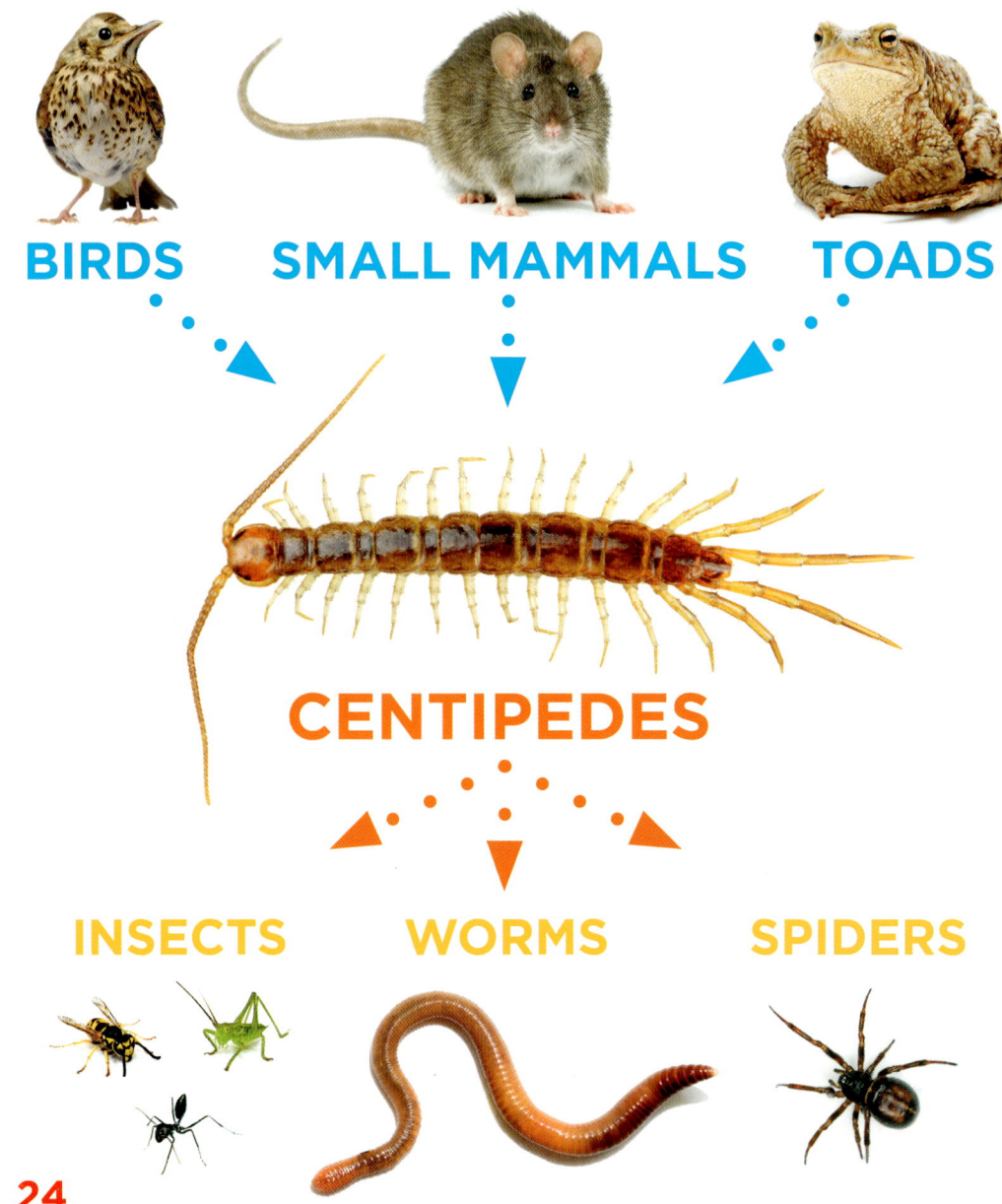

CHAPTER 4
THEIR ROLES in the World

Centipedes can protect themselves from predators. They fight with their poisonous claws. When a predator grabs a leg, a centipede might let the attacker have it. The centipede then runs away on its others. Birds, toads, and small mammals still eat many centipedes, though.

An Important Part

Some people think centipedes look awful. They call them pests and kill them. Centipedes might be creepy. But they are a big part of their **ecosystems**. Many animals rely on them for food. House centipedes eat harmful pests, such as bedbugs too.

When some centipedes lose a leg, they grow another.

BY THE NUMBERS

UP TO
6 years
LIFE SPAN

10 times
how often some centipedes molt while growing

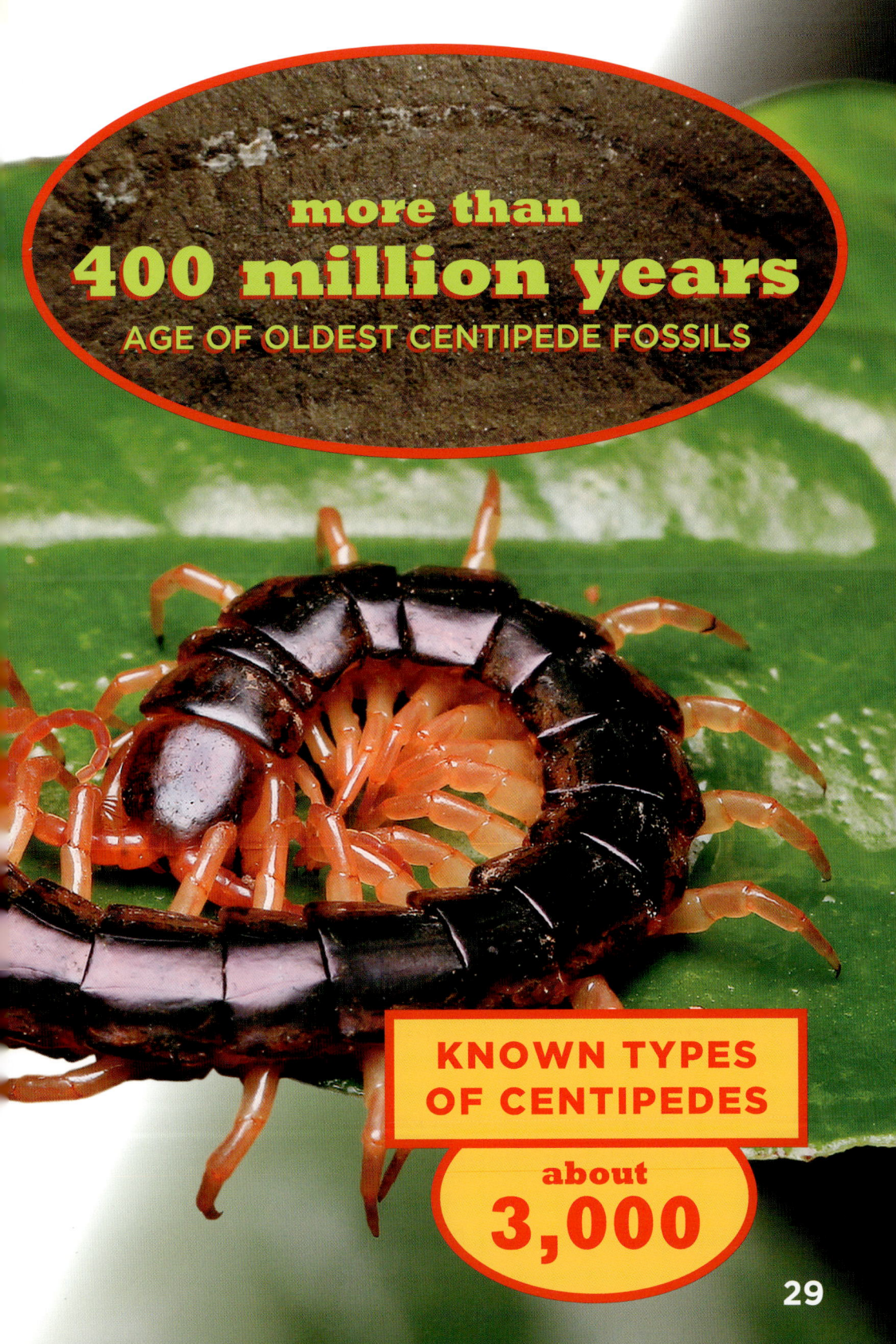

GLOSSARY

arthropod (AHR-thruh-pod)—any of a large group of animals, such as crabs, insects, and spiders, with jointed limbs and a body made up of segments

compost (KOM-pohst)—decayed organic material, such as leaves and grass, used to improve soil

ecosystem (E-co-sys-tum)—a community of living things in one place

exoskeleton (ek-so-SKE-le-ten)—the hard, protective cover on the outside of an insect's or arachnid's body

fungus (FUN-gus)—a living thing, similar to a plant that has no flowers, that lives on dead or decaying things

nymph (NIMPF)—a young insect or creature that has almost the same form as the adult

predator (PRED-uh-tuhr)—an animal that eats other animals

prey (PRAY)—an animal hunted or killed for food

segment (SEG-ment)—one of the parts into which something can be divided

spiracle (SPIR-uh-kuhl)—an opening on the body used for breathing

LEARN MORE

BOOKS
Nelson, Robin. *Speedy Centipedes.* Backyard Critters. Minneapolis: Lerner Publications, 2017.

Schuetz, Kari. *Centipedes.* Creepy Crawlies. Minneapolis: Bellwether Media, 2016.

Turner, Matt. *Tiny Creepy Crawlers.* Crazy Creepy Crawlers. Minneapolis: Hungry Tomato, 2017.

WEBSITES
Centipedes and Millipedes
easyscienceforkids.com/all-about-centipedes-and-millipedes/

Centipedes and Millipedes Facts
www.coolkidfacts.com/centipedes-and-millipedes-facts/

Centipede Facts for Kids
sciencing.com/centipede-kids-8527849.html

INDEX

B
body parts, 4, 7, 8–9, 16, 20, 25, 26

E
eggs, 18, 19, 22–23

F
food, 4, 15, 16, 24, 26

H
habitats, 4, 10–11, 12–13, 15

L
life span, 28

N
nymphs, 19, 20, 23

P
predators, 10, 24, 25, 26

S
senses, 16

sizes, 6–7, 15